ADORABLE TOWN

A FEW SINCERE WORDS FOR YOU

We appreciate you picking our coloring book amongst so many others. Your feedback is the highest compliment and source of motivation we could have acquired although we are aware that there are brilliant authors, who have written and released other excellent books.

BEFORE YOU GO

We hope you love our books and would genuinely appreciate it if you could share the sections you colored on social networks with the hashtags: #southernlotus #southernlotuscoloringbook #southernlotuscoloring

In addition, we are eager to read your Amazon reviews. We value all constructive comments, and we'll take them into careful consideration as we work to enhance both our books and our community.

Please feel free to reach out to us if you have any questions.
coloring@southernlotus.com

Visit our social media pages and follow us by using the code below:

THIS BOOK BELONGS TO

TEST COLOR PAGE

TEST COLOR PAGE

RAMEN

COFFE

OPEN

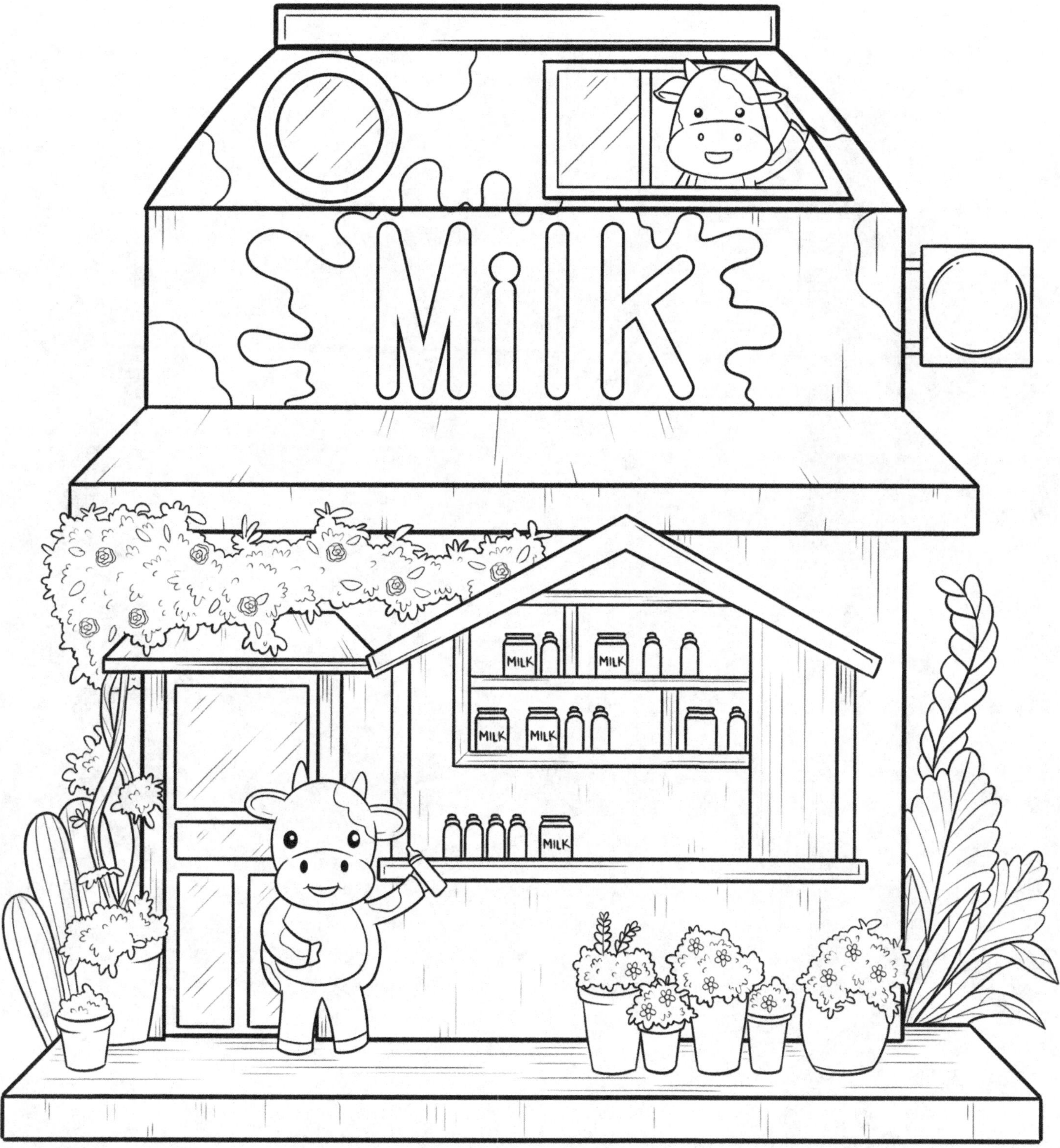
MiLK
MILK
MILK
MILK
MILK
MILK
MILK

tailor shop

Cassettes

HAMBURGER

OPEN

CReaM

Donut

Hotdog

GAME
OPEN

MILK TEA

Pizza
PIZZA

Studio

1 2 3 i
4 5 6 K
7 8 9
* 0 #

BEER

BOOKSTORE

FRIED CHICKEN

Forest Fairies

The Secret of Flowers

Beauty Witches

Love IS BEING Stupid TOGETHER

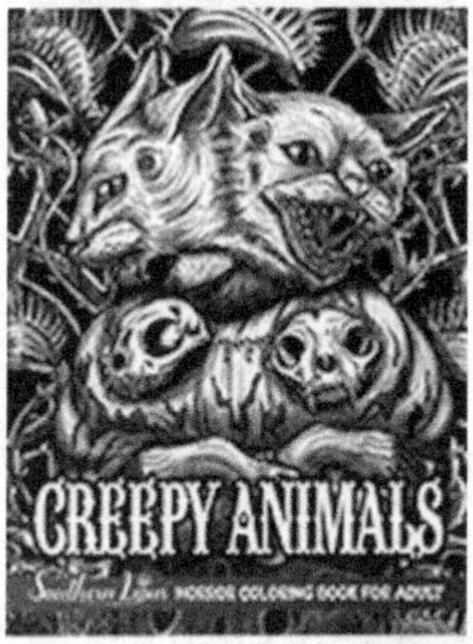
CREEPY ANIMALS

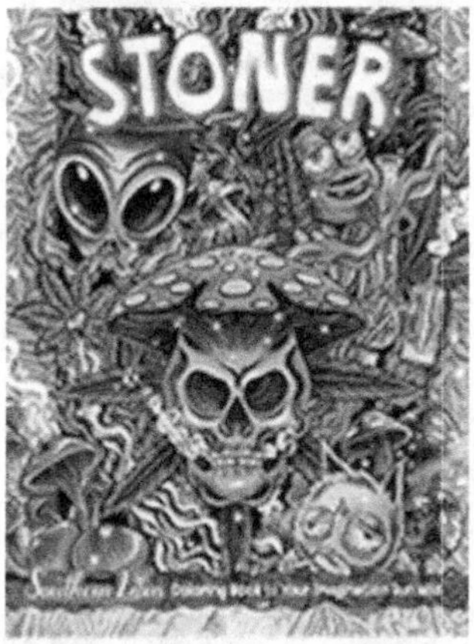
STONER

CREEPY DOLL

LITTLE CREEPY

Cozy Kitchen

POCKET ROOM

WORLD INSIDE JAR

50 Animals

UNICORN
COLORING BOOK

OUTER SPACE

ADORABLE THINGS

CREEPY FANTASY

Made in the USA
Las Vegas, NV
12 June 2023

73335272R00044